enter
or a
32
e of
..essor,
Queen Lili'uokalani, it was where the leading men and women of the Hawaiian Islands met and mingled with distinguished visitors from overseas. Princes and prelates, diplomats and naval officers, writers and artists, entrepreneurs and adventurers were welcomed and entertained with typical Hawaiian *aloha*.

The Hawaiian monarchy was established by Kamehameha I in 1796. It lasted until 1893, when it was overthrown in the reign of Queen Lili'uokalani and replaced first by a Provisional Government and then by the Republic of Hawai'i. In 1898 the Hawaiian Islands were annexed to the United States as a territory, and in 1959 the Territory of Hawai'i became the 50th state of the United States of America.

After the end of the Hawaiian monarchy in 1893, the Palace was converted into legislative halls and executive offices. The business of government continued to be conducted in the Palace until a State capitol was completed adjacent to the Palace grounds in 1969. After extensive restoration, 'Iolani Palace was reopened to the public in 1978 as a historic house museum, once again reflecting the regal grandeur that existed there during the days of the monarchy.

The Coat of Arms of the Hawaiian Kingdom bears the motto, "Ua mau ke ea o ka 'aina i ka pono," which means "The life of the land is perpetuated in righteousness."

1

A Glimpse of Hawaiian History

The history of the chiefs of Hawai'i and of the Hawaiian people stretches back over a thousand years to the time when the first Polynesians settled in the Hawaiian Islands. They were a physically robust, sea-faring people who travelled vast distances across the Pacific in outrigger canoes, sailing north from the Marquesas Islands and Tahiti in the South Pacific. Once ashore, as skilled farmers, fishermen and woodsmen, they adapted themselves to the new land and climate

The Coronation Regalia arrived from England just in time for the coronation of King Kalākaua and Queen Kapi'olani on February 12, 1883. There were two crowns of solid gold with a Hawaiian taro leaf motif, studded with diamonds, opals, emeralds, rubies and pearls. The royal scepter, symbol of peace; the sword of state, representing justice; and the gold coronation ring engraved with the Hawaiian coat of arms set off with brilliants completed the regalia ordered from abroad.

of Hawai'i and became self-reliant and self-sufficient.

Living in semi-isolation, these Polynesian pioneers developed a distinctive culture which was complex and sophisticated. Their social system was based on status, class and family; the *maka'āinana*, the people, accorded their leaders, the *ali'i*, unquestioning authority and almost god-like reverence.

When the first British explorers reached the Hawaiian Islands, they discovered that the chiefs of the various islands of the Hawaiian chain were at war with each other. In the two decades that followed the arrival of the westerners, civil war abated as Kamehameha, a chief of the Island of Hawai'i, defeated his rivals and gradually unified the islands through military might and diplomatic negotiation.

By 1810 Kamehameha had created the Hawaiian Kingdom, and before his death, in 1819, he guided his people through a period of transition from rule by many chiefs to a single ruler, from isolation to constant contact with foreigners from many lands, and

from a subsistence economy to a market economy.

Kamehameha I was succeeded by his sons, Kamehameha II, who ruled from 1819 to 1824, and Kamehameha III, from 1824 to 1854. In the early decades of the monarchy the capital of the Hawaiian kingdom was wherever the King was living — in Kailua on the Island of Hawai'i, at Waikīkī on O'ahu or at Lahaina on Maui. It was not until 1845 that Kamehameha III chose Honolulu for his permanent capital.

At that time the finest house in Honolulu belonged to the Governor of O'ahu, High Chief Mataio Kekūanaō'a. He had built it close to the harbor and near an ancient *heiau* or temple, on land which is now within the walls of 'Iolani Palace. When Kamehameha III moved to Honolulu, the Governor's mansion was turned over to the monarch. It became the royal Palace, the official residence of the Kings of Hawai'i and the focus of political and social life on O'ahu.

When Kamehameha III died, in 1854, he was succeeded by his nephew, Alexander Liholiho, the

The old 'Iolani Palace, royal residence of the Kings of Hawai'i from 1845 to 1874, was the home of Kamehameha IV and Queen Emma during their eight-year reign and it was in an adjacent bungalow that, in 1858, Queen Emma gave birth to a son, Albert Edward Kauikeaouli Leiopapa o Kamehameha. The Prince of Hawai'i, a bright and attractive youngster, was the pride and joy of his parents and the nation. In this portrait by Enoch Wood Perry, done about 1864, the Prince and his pet dogs dominate the old Palace, as the boy did during his short life. He died of a fever when he was only four years old.

Seth Joel
Bishop Museum

Christine Takata
Bishop Museum

son of Kīna'u, a *kuhina nui* or prime minister under Kamehameha III and her husband, Kekūanaō'a. He reigned as Kamehameha IV. After their wedding at Kawaiaha'o Church, in June of 1856, the young King escorted his lovely bride, Emma, across King Street to their official residence in the Palace.

By that time there were a number of buildings within the Palace grounds. The royal couple actually lived in one of them, surrounded by the homes of their retainers. The Palace itself was reserved for official functions and splendid parties, and the royal couple entertained lavishly and with great style.

Kamehameha V succeeded his brother in 1863. It was he who named his official residence 'Iolani Palace. 'Io, the high-flying Hawaiian hawk, the most majestic bird to grace the skies of the Islands, and *lani*, heaven and royalty, combined as 'Iolani, the royal or heavenly hawk. 'Iolani Palace seemed to be an appropriate name for the home of the Kings of Hawai'i. The Hawaiian hawk may occasionally be seen today gliding over the mountains of the Island of Hawai'i.

Kamehameha V, the last ruler of the Kamehameha Dynasty, left no heir to the throne. In 1873, a cousin, William Charles Lunalilo, became the first elected King of Hawai'i. His reign lasted only thirteen months, and as he left no heirs either, a second election was held, in 1874, to choose a successor. After a short but stormy campaign, the High Chief David La'amea Kalākaua won the election over the rival candidate, the Dowager Queen Emma, widow of Kamehameha IV.

King Kalākaua

Kalākaua was born on November 16, 1836. He was educated at the Chiefs' Children's School along with Kamehameha IV, Kamehameha V, Lunalilo, Queen Emma and the future Queen Lili'uokalani. He was appointed to the House of Nobles when he was twenty, and as he matured he was accorded every opportunity to participate in the government of the Kingdom. As military aide to Kamehameha IV he escorted the Duke of Edinburgh, a younger son of Queen Victoria of Great Britain, on a tour of Hawai'i, and later, as secretary of the Privy Council and Chamberlain for Kamehameha V, Kalākaua met every foreign visitor of note who visited the Islands.

Kalākaua was fluent in English as well as Hawaiian, and he was also a talented musician who wrote the words to *Hawai'i Pono'ī*, which became the Hawaiian national anthem, and the words and music to many other Hawaiian songs. He was seriously concerned about the decline of the native Hawaiian population and of many aspects of Hawaiian culture, particularly ancient forms of dance, music and historical tradition. He wrote *Legends and Myths of Hawaii* and fostered the study and enjoyment of the culture of his ancestors.

In 1863, Kalākaua married Kapi'olani, the granddaughter of Kaumuali'i, the last King of Kaua'i. They had no children of their own, but the royal couple were close to the King's sisters, Likelike and Lili'uokalani, and to the Queen's sisters, Po'omaikelani and Kino'iki Kekaulike, and to their children, Likelike's daughter Ka'iulani and Kekaulike's sons Edward Keli'iahonui, Jonah

George E. Bacon

Kalaniana'ole and David Kawānanakoa.

During the first winter of his rule, 1874–75, Kalākaua travelled to the United States. He met and was entertained by President Ulysses S. Grant and prominent American politicians and officials, as he worked to achieve his main objective, the economic security of his Kingdom. He was invited to address the Congress of the United States, the first king to be so honored, and he spoke out on the need for a trade agreement between the United States and Hawai'i. During his short stay in Washington, D.C., he engendered so much good will towards Hawai'i that the Congress agreed to pass a U.S.-Hawai'i reciprocity treaty which had been under

negotiation for some twenty-five years. This was the important treaty which allowed Hawaiian sugar to enter the American market free of duty and was vital to the future economic well-being of the Hawaiian Kingdom.

King Kalākaua, in full dress uniform, wearing the four Hawaiian orders, the stars of Kalākaua, Kapi'olani, Kamehameha I and the Crown of Hawai'i and six foreign orders given him by the rulers of Belgium, Denmark, Germany, Great Britain, Japan and Sweden. Beside him are the crown and scepter of Hawai'i, and on his hand is his gold coronation ring. The portrait was painted in 1891 by an American artist, William Cogswell (1819–1903), and hangs in the Blue Room.

The New Palace

While Kalākaua was on the U.S. mainland coping with affairs of state, he entrusted to his brother-in-law, Archibald S. Cleghorn, the task of sprucing up the old Palace and its grounds. With $16,000 appropriated by the Hawaiian legislature, Cleghorn supervised the demolition of a number of subsidiary buildings in the royal compound and the renovation of others, but he soon discovered that at the Palace the termites had triumphed. The aging structure was in such poor condition that the thrifty Scot decided that it would be a waste to spend any more money on it, and he ordered it torn down.

When King Kalākaua returned from his travels he was warmly welcomed by his people but, according to the contemporary newspaper accounts, was taken by surprise when he viewed the transformation which had taken place within the Palace grounds:

all that was left of his Palace was the foundation. The King had to move temporarily into one of his personal homes.

It took a few years for the King to persuade the legislature to appropriate enough money to build a new official residence, but, in 1880, $50,000 was set aside for the construction of the second 'Iolani Palace. Building costs escalated over the next few years, and by 1884, $343,545 had been spent on the royal residence.

On December 31, 1879, the forty-fifth birthday of Queen Kapi'olani, the cornerstone of the Palace was laid with full Masonic rites. A copper casket containing memorabilia of the day was inserted into a hollowed-out concrete block, and as the Royal Hawaiian Band played solemn music, the cornerstone was lowered into place, and King Kalākaua and the Masonic Grand Master descended into the excavations to supervise the elaborate ritual.

This ceremony is recorded in detail in contemporary newspapers and Masonic accounts, but today a mystery surrounds the event, for when the restoration of the Palace was undertaken in 1969, the cornerstone could not be found. Architects poured over the blueprints, archeologists probed the foundations and the U.S. Army even assigned its metal detection squad to assist in the search—but the cornerstone has still not been located.

The new 'Iolani Palace was set in the midst of spacious grounds. In this photograph, taken during the 1880s, the landscaped grounds and the row of royal palms are just beginning to take hold. To the left of the picture is the Bungalow, an informal residence for the King and Queen. The Bungalow was torn down in 1919 and, in 1965, the 'Iolani Barracks, shown at the extreme right of the picture, was moved from the grounds of the new capitol to its present site in the Palace grounds.

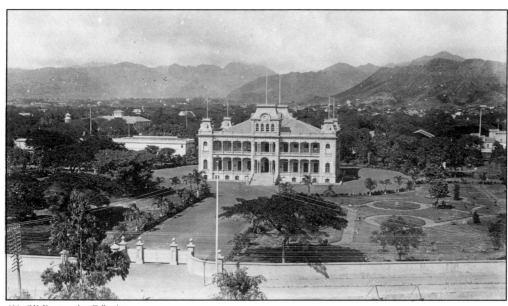

Abigail K. Kawananakoa Collection

Building a Palace

Four architects had a hand in the drawings for the new Palace. The first, Thomas Rowe of Sydney, Australia, won a worldwide competition to design a royal residence for Honolulu, but in 1871 the Hawaiian legislature was not ready to appropriate the funds needed to build such an imposing building. Instead, they had Rowe's plans altered and erected a government office building, Ali'iōlani Hale, on a site across King Street from the Palace. Eight years later, when more money was available and the old Palace had been demolished, Rowe's drawings were resurrected and readapted to the requirements of a royal residence by Thomas J. Baker, an architect temporarily living in Honolulu.

Early in 1880, Charles J. Wall, a San Francisco architect, finished the drawings for the Palace. The final responsibility for supervising construction was given to Isaac Moore, a draftsman at the Honolulu Planing Mill. He worked closely with the Superintendent of Public Works, Robert Stirling, who was in overall control of supplies, labor and general work schedules, assisted by another Englishman, Edward Bedford Thomas, who was both the on-site supervisor of the work and in charge of bricklaying.

The Palace was built largely by local contractors, artisans and laborers, but much of the material used was imported. Redwood and Port Orford cedar were imported from the Pacific Northwest, sheets of etched glass for the doors of the main hall and plate glass for the other doors and the windows arrived from San Francisco, as did the cast iron columns that line the verandas. Also from California came two dumbwaiters, small elevators operated by ropes and pulleys and used to convey food from the kitchen in the basement to the dining room on the first

On the front veranda the plaster and cement work, both decorative and plain, which covers the basic brick walls inside and on the facing and outer walls, was done by the Honolulu firm of John Bowler and Company. The iron balustrades of the upper verandah were fabricated by the Honolulu Iron Works and the cast iron columns were sent to the Islands from San Francisco. Wooden casts for the Hawaiian coat of arms and the other panels on the ceilings of the verandas were handcrafted by a Chinese woodworker, Chun Moke (Mo-ke). Mirrors served to enhance the electric lights. Two massive bronze vases that flanked the main entrance were presented to King Kalākaua by the Chinese community on the occasion of his coronation in 1883.

floor and the private apartments on the second. Slate for the roof was shipped all the way from a quarry in Pennsylvania.

The architectural style of the new Palace has been called "American Florentine," but with its solid bulk and deep verandas, high ceilings and proliferation of doors and windows it bears a close resemblance to many of the important governmental-colonial residences erected in tropical and subtropical countries during the late Victorian period.

King Kalākaua took an active interest in the construction of his new Palace, and it was at his instigation that many "progressive" elements were included. For example, in the early 1880s, the use of concrete was new to masons throughout the world, but several experts in this modern building technique had been brought to Hawai'i by the Hawaiian government ten years earlier to work on Ali'iōlani Hale and were still in Honolulu.

The plumbing arrangements were lavish. On the second floor there were four full bathrooms, an almost unheard-of luxury in the 1880s. The King's copper-lined bathtub was 7 feet long, 2 feet wide and 2 feet deep. No expense was spared in providing the most modern of plumbing throughout the building. The wash basins were of Italian marble. Off the dining room were two "water closets" for guests, and in the spacious butler's pantry copper sinks and running water were installed. In the basement there were deep sinks in the kitchen and laundry rooms, and the staff was provided with a bathtub, shower (with cold water) and toilets.

The new Palace was initially provided with gas chandeliers, the most modern lighting at that time. But in 1881, on his trip around the world, the King was enthralled with a display of electric lights which he saw in Paris. This was even more up-to-date. Kalākaua resolved to import electricity into the Hawaiian Islands immediately and use his Palace as a showplace for this latest marvel.

Less than seven years after Thomas A. Edison invented the first practical incandescent bulb, arc lights were displayed on the exterior verandas of 'Iolani Palace for the royal jubilee celebrating the King's 50th birthday in November of 1886. In 1887 electricity was installed in the main rooms of the Palace. The people of Hawai'i were as enthusiastic about the new invention as was their King, and within a few years the streets and homes of Honolulu also glowed with electricity.

The King installed a modern communications system. In 1876, the telephone was invented by Alexander Graham Bell, and two years later Charles H. Dickey of Ha'ikū, Maui, introduced the new invention into the Islands. Intrigued with the new gadget, Princess Likelike ordered a telephone from San Francisco for her brother.

In 1880, the Hawaiian Bell Telephone Company was organized in the Islands by Charles O. Berger, and a telephone was immediately installed in the Palace. It consisted of a telephone box which was attached to the wall and a single instrument used for both speaking and hearing, but it allowed the King to talk to the Queen in her apartments across the hall. A replica of a "more modern" 1883 telephone, on which the King could give instructions to the chamberlain in his office in

George E. Bacon

Sheet crystal door panels were made in England and designed and etched in San Francisco for the massive front and rear portals of the Palace. The Hawaiian Consul in San Francisco, Henry W. Severance, in 1881 wrote a bit apprehensively to the Minister of the Interior in Honolulu: " The workmen who executed the figured glass, are inclined to decorate profusely but I have tried to keep them within limits. I hope in your judgment they have not exceeded the bounds of good taste in the figures represented. In the large Transom lights which have the coat of arms, I wished to have the Taro leaf introduced, which is similar to the leaf of the Calla lily, but in making the same they have added the flower. I shall be glad to know that you approve all the work."

the basement and chat with his friends through the city system, is exhibited in the King's library.

Another innovation which the King incorporated into his plans for the Palace was the use of water from an artesian well. This method of obtaining water had first been tried on Oʻahu in 1879. In 1883, the McCandless brothers, a team of well drillers, struck a vein of artesian water at 730 feet, at the rear of the Palace. This new source of water eventually supplied the needs of the royal household and, through mains, the entire neighborhood. The original well, near the gate between the Palace grounds and the Capitol, was covered in 1921 with a fountain-like structure.

In August of 1882, Kalākaua held his first big entertainment in the new Palace, a luncheon for the members of the legislature at the conclusion of their 1882 session. The *Honolulu Daily Bulletin* described the party as "informal and jolly." The informality may have stemmed from the fact that the furniture for the Palace did not arrive in Honolulu from Boston until about three weeks after the luncheon.

Four months later, King Kalākaua and Queen Kapiʻolani moved into their new Palace. From then until the King's death in 1891 and throughout the reign of his successor, his sister Queen Liliʻuokalani, ʻIolani Palace was the formal residence of the kings and queens of Hawaiʻi. It was not their only home, for like most rulers and heads of state they had a number of other dwellings within their realm, but the Palace was the focal point of the political and social life of the Kingdom of Hawaiʻi.

Approaching the Palace

Wide carriage drives have been constructed from the King Street and Richard Street gates. They sweep entirely around the Palace. In front they broaden into a great oval affording room for a muster of the Household Troops and the Band on State occasions without interference with the approach for carriages.

Visitors of King Kalākaua drew up before the King Street entrance of the Palace in their carriages. Royal servants took charge of their horses and rigs, while the formally dressed guests mounted the iron steps and crossed the spacious veranda to massive double doors. As the glass-paneled portals were opened, newcomers invariably paused to examine the figures and symbols etched in the glass, specially designed in San Francisco to the King's taste.

In the Grand Hall handsome Hawaiian woods provide a fitting background for a display of Hawaiian history. Niches on both side walls contain gifts to King Kalākaua and in a row above are oil portraits of the Kings and Queens of Hawaiʻi.

The carpentry throughout the Palace was supervised by George Lucas of the Honolulu Steam Planing Mill. For the decorative woodwork he used a magnificent array of native Hawaiian woods: koa, kou and kamani.

MILROY/McALEER

9

The Grand Hall

Ten portraits of past kings and queens of Hawai'i hung on the walls of the Grand Hall, as they do now. Immediately to the right of the entrance is the portrait of Kamehameha I, painted in 1850 by a visiting American artist, James Gay Sawkins. Beside it is a painting of the High Chiefess Kekāuluohi, one of the last wives of Kamehameha I. Her portrait, completed in the 1850s, is attributed to Charles Bird King, a well-known Washington, D.C., portraitist.

In the center of the wall to the right of the front door are a pair of portraits of Kamehameha II and his favorite wife, Kamāmalu, which were painted in 1825 by a young French artist Eugénie Lebrun. Paintings of Kamehameha III and Queen Kalama, done by another American, John Mix Stanley, during a visit to Hawai'i in 1849, are closest to the rear entrance doors. The glass panels in these doors are also etched with figures and flowers and the royal coat of arms.

On the wall to the left of the entrance, starting at the rear of the Palace, is the portrait of Queen Emma, wife of Kamehameha IV, which is attributed to Charles Hasselmann, and beside it is a painting of Kamehameha IV, thought to have been done by William Cogswell, a well-known American artist. Cogswell may also have painted the likeness of Kamehameha V, but as neither canvas is signed we can only speculate. Closest to the front entrance is a painting of William Charles Lunalilo, the first elected monarch of Hawai'i, rendered by a Danish artist, Eiler Andreas Chrisoffer Jurgensen.

Below these historic portraits, in niches on either wall of the Grand Hall, are displayed valuable objects from overseas: porcelain vases from England and Japan, brass from India and statuettes from France. In the days of the monarchy, the Grand Hall was often filled with elaborate floral arrangements, banks of ferns and flowers adding their color and beauty to the polished woodwork and the works of art.

The main staircase rises dramatically from the main floor. It was constructed by Hawaiian carpenters of koa wood with kamani and walnut trim. The koa stair treads are the only original flooring in the Palace. Some of the balusters had been eaten by termites and had to be replaced during restoration.

The Blue Room

On informal occasions the visitor would be ushered into the Blue Room, immediately to the left of the main entrance to the Palace. Here were held small receptions, casual gatherings, and it was in this room that visitors often assembled before state audiences in the Throne Room. Comfortably furnished with chairs and sofas upholstered in blue, the room was dominated by a grand piano. It was often the scene of musicales, for most of the members of the Hawaiian royal family were not only competent musicians but rejoiced in evenings of music.

Their Majesties gave the first of a series of musicals at Iolani Palace. It was held in the blue room which was most tastily decorated with potted ferns and palms, and flowers. The folding doors between the blue room and the dining hall were thrown open, and chairs placed in the latter room were occupied by the invited guests.

It was here in the Blue Room that, on January 14, 1893, Queen Lili'uokalani gathered her cabinet ministers about her and presented to them a new constitution, designed to restore her royal prerogatives. Her announcement that she proposed to sign this constitution precipitated the overthrow of the monarchy.

The heavy draperies in the Blue Room, the informal reception room, are of blue satin trimmed with velvet, over lace bordered glass curtains. Most of the furniture was from the old 'Iolani Palace. The large portrait of Louis Philippe of France was a gift from that ruler to Kamehameha III. It was painted in the studio of the famous German portraitist, Franz-Xavier Winterhalter, and arrived in the Hawaiian islands in 1848. During the reign of Queen Lili'uokalani, a large portrait of King Kalākaua and the two shown above, of the Queen and her consort, John Owen Dominis, all by William Cogswell, also hung in the Blue Room.

State Dining Room

The heavily carved pair of sliding doors which divide the Blue Room from the Dining Room are of koa wood with kamani wood panels and walnut moulding.

The Dining Room must have had a very grand appearance when State dinners were held there. The King and Queen, elegant in evening dress and decorations, would be seated in capacious chairs, which were upholstered in soft leather and topped with carved royal crowns. They presided over long tables which could accommodate forty guests, each lady or gentleman handsomely attired in silken gown or dress uniform and attended by liveried footmen.

The tables were adorned with flowers in silver vases, a massive epergne and several candelabra, supplemented by "pretty fairy lamps." To honor a visiting American admiral, a centerpiece was created in the shape of an anchor three feet tall composed entirely of roses, shaded from deep red to white and placed on a base of crimson silk. During dinner the Royal Hawaiian Band, stationed on the veranda outside the Dining Room windows, entertained the guests with waltzes, polkas and excerpts from operas.

The chairs, tables and sideboards in the Dining Room were all built by A. H. Davenport & Co. of Boston, Massachusetts, as was much of the furniture in the Palace. Most of the pieces are carved with a distinctive quatre-foil design, typical of Gothic-Revival furniture of the late Victorian period, and upholstered in a variety of rich fabrics and leathers, fit for a king. On the walls of the State Dining Room hung portraits of European royalty, sent to the Kings of Hawai'i by the crowned heads of France, Prussia and Russia. These European monarchs were well aware of the strategic position of Hawai'i in the North Pacific, realized the importance of access to Honolulu's excellent harbor and valued the warm welcome accorded the sailors of the world by the Hawaiian people. Foreign ships were frequent visitors to Hawaiian waters, and most of the major nations of the world had treaties of commerce and friendship with the island kingdom.

The earliest portrait arrived in Honolulu in 1830. Kamehameha III had sent Frederick William III of Prussia several feather cloaks and in return received a number of gifts including portraits of the King of Prussia and his favorite Field Marshal, Count Gebhard Leberecht von Blücher, a hero of the battle of Waterloo.

In 1847, Frederick William IV, who had succeeded his father as King of Prussia, sent his own portrait to Kamehameha III, and the following year, King Louis Philippe of France dispatched a huge portrait of himself to Hawai'i. That same year, a portrait of Rear Admiral Richard D. Thomas, R.N., arrived from England. Admiral Thomas was highly respected by Kamehameha III and the Hawaiian people.

The Admiral Thomas story starts in 1843, when a young British naval officer, Lord Paulet, in an effort to redress wrongs allegedly suffered by some British subjects then living in Hawai'i exceeded his instructions. He landed English sailors at Honolulu and assumed control of the government of the kingdom. As soon as he heard of the outrage, Paulet's superior officer, Admiral Thomas, sailed from his headquarters on the coast of Chile to Hawai'i, and immediately restored to Kamehameha III and his people the independence of which they had temporarily been deprived.

Kamehameha V was the last Hawaiian monarch to receive oil paintings of European kings. In 1864 Alexander II, Czar of all the Russias, sent him his portrait, and six years later he received a likeness of Napoleon III.

On a table in the State Dining Room is an ornate bronze and ormolu clock, one of the gifts to Kamehameha IV from Emperor Napoleon III of France, whose portrait hangs on the inner wall of the room. Made by E. Vittoz & Cie of Paris, the clock is set in an ormolu globe encircled by a band of astrological signs in slight relief. The clock is on loan to the Friends of 'Iolani Palace from the Estate of Samuel Mills Damon.

In the State Dining Room European
visitors to King Kalākaua's court
dined beneath portraits of monarchs
and distinguished men from their
homelands. Portraits of Admiral
Richard D. Thomas, R.N., Napoleon
III of France and Frederick William
IV of Prussia hang above the massive
sideboards. The table was laid with
china from France, crystal from
Bohemia and silver from England,
France, China and the United States.

The Throne Room

The Throne Room . . . was a scene of dazzling brilliancy, lighted . . . by hundreds of incandescent lamps from handsome crystal chandeliers . . . .On one side were two immense floral devices of the choicest flowers, principally roses, representing Diamond Head and Round Top. On the dais on either side were stationed **kahili** *bearers, . . .*

proudly holding their tall emblems of the Hawaiian majesty. The King and Queen stood just below the dais, with the members of the royal family on their left and their guests of honor on their right. Among King Kalākaua's royal guests were HRH Prince Oscar of Sweden, Prince Giovanni del Drago of Italy and the Prince and Princess de Bourbon. Several Japanese government delegations paused in Honolulu en route to Washington, D.C., or on their return to Tokyo and were welcomed royally by the King. A. G. Spalding and the members of his touring baseball team were among the many men and women from numerous walks of life whom the King received and entertained.

While the Royal Hawaiian Band, stationed on the veranda outside the Throne Room, played classical music, the guests filed into the spacious room singly or in couples. They bowed low to the King and Queen and those in the receiving line before greeting their friends. When all the company was assembled the King would give a signal to Bandmaster Henry Berger. His players switched to lively dance tunes, and the ball began.

The King loved to dance, and balls at 'Iolani Palace often lasted until the wee hours of the morning, with a midnight pause for

refreshments in the State Dining Room.

On musical evenings, the King's collections of feather cloaks or of Hawaiian artifacts were often placed on display in the Throne Room, and during the King's jubilee, hundreds of gifts were arranged on the floor in front of the dais, for the public to view.

The King also held formal audiences in the late morning. These affairs were often followed by what was called a "breakfast" but occurred about noon. They took place when distinguished visitors were first welcomed to the Kingdom, newly appointed diplomats presented their credentials, foreign naval officers first called at the Palace after their arrival in the harbor, government proclamations were declared, royal orders were presented to men and women who had served the Kingdom well and the people of Hawai'i came to the Palace to present petitions to the King.

There were also sad occasions in the Throne Room. After King Kalākaua died of Bright's disease in San Francisco in January of 1891, his body was returned to Honolulu aboard the USS *Charleston*. It was placed in the Throne Room of his Palace where it lay in state, the bier covered by a feather cloak, upon which were laid the King's crown, sword and scepter.

For two weeks the people of Hawai'i silently filed through the Throne Room to pay their last respects to their King, and it was there that Bishop Alfred Willis of the Anglican Church conducted the funeral service. He was accompanied by the choir of Kawaiaha'o Church, and the Eucharist was celebrated in the Hawaiian language.

Massive gilded cornices,

Escutcheons lined the walls of the Throne Room. Gilded oval frames lined with velvet and covered with locked glass doors, they were designed by the Boston jewelry firm of Shreve, Crump and Low to display four of the Hawaiian royal orders and twelve foreign orders conferred on King Kalākaua. Each escutcheon is surmounted by the coat of arms of the Kingdom of Hawai'i or the heraldic shield of the country which presented the decoration. On each side of the dais the escutcheons originally contained the orders of the Crown of Hawai'i, the Order of Kapi'olani, the Order of Kamehameha I and the Order of Kalākaua. Clockwise around the Throne Room beginning at the right of the dais, are escutcheons for orders from Japan, Austria-Hungary, Sweden and Norway, Denmark, Spain, Italy, Venezuela, Siam, Belgium, Prussia-Germany, Portugal and Great Britain.

The Throne Room has been restored to its appearance during the reign of King Kalākaua. After the overthrow of the monarchy, the thrones, the crowns, the magnificent feather cloaks which had been passed down from generation to generation in the Kamehameha family and the tall *kāhili* which were carried before Hawaiian chiefs on state occasions were all sent to the Bernice Pauahi Bishop Museum in Honolulu, where they were eventually put on display. The chandeliers, mirrors, cornices and draperies and the center sofa and side chairs have all been meticulously restored or duplicated.

Hawaii State Archives

surmounted by crossed spears, capped each of the tall windows of the Throne Room. Heavy maroon satin draperies with velvet trim and delicate lace window curtains reached the floor. The original Wilton carpet, woven in England, had a design of tropical foliage in shades of red and soft green. A duplicate carpet was especially woven for the restored Throne Room from a sample of the original and replicates the original pattern precisely.

The King's Bedroom. When the Provisional Government personnel moved in and turned the royal apartments into utilitarian government offices, they kept the chairs and tables, bookcases and desks, cabinets and mirrors and even a washstand or two. The personal possessions of Queen Lili'uokalani were returned to her while the rest of the furniture was sold at a series of public auctions between 1895 and 1903. Since the restoration of the Palace began, many pieces have been returned to the Friends of 'Iolani Palace, such as the small square stand in this picture which was donated by a resident of Oklahoma City.

The King's Bedroom

The King's bedroom was at the back, connected with a library, in which his privy council met, and at the front of the Palace was the Gold or Music Room, where the royal family entertained informally. Each bedroom had a large, Gothic-Revival bed embellished with a crown at the top of a half-canopy. The King's bed was distinguished by its ebony finish and gold tracery. The bedroom furniture also included large wardrobes and dressers, an intricately carved dressing table, arm chairs and side chairs, lounges and writing tables.

In the King's Bedroom is a small, inlaid, tilt-top table, the marquetry surface of which is designed in a star motif of a variety of Hawaiian woods. This table is thought to have been manufactured in Hawai'i. It is now back in its original position near the windows.

The Second Floor

The private quarters of the royal family were on the second floor of the Palace. To the right of the curving staircase was the King's suite and to the left the Queen's, each set of apartments consisting of three spacious rooms with dressing and bathrooms attached. The dominant color in the King's bedroom was blue, in Queen Kapi'olani's it was red and in the guest rooms yellow and blue. Tall jib windows gave onto shadowed verandas, and in each corner of the building was an informal sitting room.

The majolica vase in the center of this photograph of the King's Bedroom was made in 1867 by the English firm of Minton. It is one of only ten 'Prometheus' vases known to exist. It was preserved by the family of Prince David Kalākaua Kawananakoa, grand nephew of King Kalākaua and Queen Kapi'olani, and returned to 'Iolani Palace in 1981 by Kahauanu Lake, whose mother, Cecelia Waipa, was Prince David's widow.

The Library

Davenport furniture predominated in the Palace from the thrones to the occasional chairs. The Palace now possesses one of the most representative collections of this type of furniture in the United States, but not all the royal furnishings in the Palace bore the Davenport name. The King and Queen surrounded themselves with many older pieces of furniture brought from the former Palace or from one of their other residences. The private apartments were filled with a large collection of family memen-toes and curios from every part of the world which achieved a style of decoration popular with the gentry of the late Victorian period.

The library was furnished with a table ten feet long and five feet wide, a distinctive Davenport creation, but the chairs were high-backed Elizabethan reproductions and there were two revolving book stands constructed by a local cabinetmaker, of Hawaiian koa and walnut. Above bookcases filled with reference works and government papers, pictures of public figures and family members lined the walls.

King Kalākaua's Library was furnished by the King when he moved into the Palace in 1883. On the walls are portraits of British Prime Ministers William E. Gladstone and Benjamin Disraeli, and an 1882 lithograph of the British House of Commons. The Library, and the Chamberlain's Office in the basement, were the center of official business in the Palace. They were both restored with a generous grant from the General Telephone and Electronics Foundation and the Hawaiian Telephone Company.

Hawaii State Archives

The Gold or Music Room

At the front of the building was the Gold or Music Room where the royal family gathered for private musicales. In the center of the room was a circular sofa, upholstered in gold mohair satin, similar in general design to the sofa in the Throne Room but not so large. Tables fashioned from a variety of Hawaiian woods were piled high with sheet music, while a number of musical instruments and music racks stood ready for the royal players.

The Upper Hall

The wide hall which separated the King's suite from that of his Queen was used during the monarchy period as an upstairs sitting room, a place for the family and their friends to congregate for informal dining. A portion of the King's collection of Hawaiian artifacts was displayed in massive curio cabinets placed along the walls of the hall and on special occasions a selection of precious *tapa*, ancient Hawaiian wooden bowls and other heirlooms were exhibited there, draped over sofas and chairs and set out on tables or arranged on the floor.

George E. Bacon

Queen Kapiʻolani's Suite

The Queen's apartments consisted of a suite of three bedrooms, each with a dressing room, a bathroom and, in the two corners of the building, attractive sitting rooms. The Queen's own bedroom, opposite the King's, connected with rooms often used by her sister Poʻomaikelani, or by the young princes Edward Keliʻiahonui, Jonah Kūhiō Kalanianaʻole and David Kawananakoa, children of her younger sister, Kinoiki Kekaulike.

When the young princes were visiting, the Palace rang with happy voices and the thunder of young people racing up and down the center hall and playing hide and seek in the well-furnished rooms while their elders entertained friends in the Gold Room or strolled back and forth on the verandas in the cool of the evening.

Queen Kapiʻolani in formal attire. She is wearing the sash of the order of Kalākaua and the star of the Knights Grand Cross of the Royal Order of Kamehameha I. The photograph was taken by I. W. Taber and handtinted in polychrome by J. Koch.

Queen Kapiʻolani's bedroom contains a number of original pieces of furniture made by A. H. Davenport Company as well as personal possessions of Queen Kapiʻolani. The English style center table of intricately carved rosewood was built around 1850, and the Chinese silk bedspread and pillow shams bear the Queen's monogram.

Queen Liliʻuokalani

Born on September 2, 1838, Liliʻuokalani was less than two years younger than her brother, Kalākaua, who reigned from 1874 until 1891. Like him, she had been educated at the Chiefs' Children's School with the other royal princes and princesses. In 1862, she married her childhood sweetheart, John Owen Dominis, who was then the Governor of Oʻahu. She had a gift for languages and therefore was able to move easily in the Hawaiian and foreign communities.

During the years of her brother's reign, Liliʻuokalani had several opportunities to travel abroad. In 1878, she visited California, and in 1887 she accompanied Queen Kapiʻolani on a trip to the United States and to England, where the two royal ladies attended the Jubilee celebrations for Queen Victoria. She also served as regent for her brother twice, the first time during his world tour in 1881 and again in 1890–91 when he visited the United States, and learned at first hand the problems of ruling a Kingdom. By the time she came to the throne in January of 1891, Liliʻuokalani had had a good deal of training for her new role— Queen of Hawaiʻi.

The two years of her reign were an unusually difficult time for the Hawaiian Kingdom. The sugar industry, the mainstay of the Hawaiian economy, was in the doldrums, tax revenues had decreased, and the Kingdom had serious financial difficulties. A few months after she assumed the monarchy her trusted advisor, her husband, died. Many of her subsequent advisors were neither experienced nor wise.

Her economic and political problems, however, had deep roots over which she had no control. Pressures, both external and internal, which had been brought to bear on the monarchy since the reign of Kamehameha I, had built up to serious proportions during the Queen's tenure. In spite of her efforts to strengthen the declining political position of the monarchy and to limit the franchise to Hawaiian-born or naturalized male subjects by promulgating a new Constitution, the opposition to her wishes grew so strong that it was no longer possible for her to rule effectively.

In January of 1893 Queen Liliʻuokalani had no alternative other than to surrender the administration of her Kingdom to a group of pro-annexationist Honolulu businessmen who promptly formed a provisional government. The Queen stepped down under protest, laying the blame for her overthrow on U.S. Minister John L. Stevens who "caused United States troops to be landed at Honolulu and declared that he would support the said provisional government." She was confident, however, that the government of the United States would respond favorably to her plea for restoration as Queen of Hawaiʻi.

Her case was listened to with sympathy both in Honolulu and Washington, but the United States government, after sending commissioners to investigate the situation in Hawaiʻi, refused to take overt action to oust the Provisional Government or to restore the Queen to her throne. When the Provisional Government learned that the government of the United States would neither restore the monarchy nor annex the Hawaiian Islands to the United

George E. Bacon

Queen Lili'uokalani painted by William Cogswell in 1891. The Queen is wearing the star, cross and sash of the Knights Grand Cross of the Order of Kalākaua. In her hair is a diamond butterfly pin which she purchased while in London in 1887.

States as the Provisional Government desired, it reconstituted itself as the Republic of Hawai'i, confident that the next administration in Washington, D.C., would approve annexation, as it did.

In 1893, Queen Lili'uokalani retired to her residence at Washington Place, which is now the Governor's Mansion. There she was surrounded by royalists, some of whom were determined to restore the monarchy. After an abortive uprising by native Hawaiian monarchists against the Republic of Hawai'i in 1895, the Queen was arrested, confined and brought to trial in what had been her Throne Room. She was found guilty of having concealed from the authorities her knowledge of the intentions of the rebels who had risen against the Republic and was imprisoned in an upstairs bedroom of 'Iolani Palace. When she was released, in September of 1895, she returned to Washington Place, where she lived until her death in 1917.

Queen Lili'uokalani's Prison Chamber

Lili'uokalani's room was sparsely furnished with only the bare necessities. Her meals were prepared in her own kitchen at Washington Place and brought to her in her prison by her steward, and the former Queen was allowed to have only one of her ladies with her during the day. It

was a lonely but not unproductive life, for *"though I was still not allowed to have newspapers or general literature to read, writing-paper and lead-pencils were not denied; and I was thereby able to write music, after drawing for myself the lines of the staff. ... I found great consolation in composing, and transcribed a number of songs, ..."*

It was here in her prison room that Lili'uokalani composed the words and music of the lovely *"Queen's Prayer."* Two stanzas describe her anguish, her Christian charity and her trust in God.

Ko'u noho mihi 'ana
A pa'ahao 'ia
'O 'oe ku'u lama,
Kou nani, ko'u ko'o

Mai nānā 'ino'ino
Nā hewa o kānaka,
Aka e huikala
A ma'ema'e nō.

I live in sorrow
Imprisoned,
You are my light,
Your glory my support.

Behold not with malevolence
The sins of man,
But forgive
And cleanse.

The Basement

The basement quarters were probably the liveliest rooms in the entire Palace since it was from a basement office that the chamberlain supervised the operation of the whole household.

On either side of the wide central corridor were rooms for the forty to sixty servants, some of whom were constantly on duty. Here could also be found the spacious storerooms in which were kept the *kāhili*, the tall

feather-topped staffs borne before Hawaiian royalty, the silver, the wines and all the things needed by the Palace staff for a continuous and varied round of events.

As originally designed, the basement rooms would have been dark, with only small, high windows, but the fortuitous addition of a walled dry moat around the entire building allowed the architect to add full-sized windows to the basement rooms, providing needed light and air.

The Executive Building

After the overthrow of the monarchy in 1893, the Palace was converted into a government office building and renamed The Executive Building. The Territorial Senate met in the State Dining Room and the House of Representatives in the Throne Room. Heavy safes were moved into the Blue Room for the Minister of Finance, while the Registrar of Public Accounts did business through one of the veranda windows.

Upstairs, President Sanford B. Dole, later Governor Dole, and his successors, used the King's bedroom and library, the Minister of Foreign Affairs moved into the Gold Room and the Attorney General was allotted Queen Kapi'olani's bedroom. After Queen Lili'uokalani was released from imprisonment in the Palace, the executive staff spread into that area also, and for many years it was the office of the Secretary of the Territory and, later, the Lieutenant Governor of the State of Hawai'i.

Aerial view of the Palace, its grounds and the State Capitol, on following page. *Photo:* Hawaiian Service, Inc.

Restoring a Palace

Hawai'i became a territory of the United States of America in 1898, and in 1959 the 50th state of the union. During all those years 'Iolani Palace was used by the Governor and his staff and by the Legislature of the Territorial and State governments until, in 1969, Governor John A. Burns and his administration moved into the new capitol adjacent to the Palace grounds.

In 1938 the Throne Room was restored and a number of internal supporting beams replaced, but it was only in 1969 that a full-scale restoration of the Palace was begun. The floors, walls and ceilings had to be completely stripped, plumbing and electric wiring were rerouted and steel members were inserted where needed to insure the stability of the structure. Once the architects and builders were assured that the Palace was sound, new wooden floors were installed, walls and ceilings were replaced and a master plasterer was brought out of retirement in Italy to duplicate the monarchy period decorative plaster designs on the ceilings. Slowly the Palace was restored to its former grandeur.

Before that time, however, a good deal of ground work had already been done on plans for restoration. Mrs. Lili'uokalani Kawananakoa Morris, a grand-niece of Queen Kapi'olani and

Hawaii State Archives

daughter of David Kawananakoa, one of the last royal princes of Hawai'i, founded a community-based organization, The Friends of 'Iolani Palace, which was dedicated to the restoration of the Palace and the preservation of the history of the Hawaiian monarchy. Since the death of Mrs. Morris, her work has been carried on by other members of the Hawaiian royal family, most recently by her daughter, Abigail Kekaulike Kawananakoa.

In 1965 the Junior League of Honolulu funded and staffed a scholarly investigation into the construction, decoration and furnishing of the Palace and the planting of the grounds during the late monarchy period. Members of the League's research committee combed old inventories, government records and the newspapers of the latter part of the 19th century in an effort to assemble an accurate picture of what the Palace had been like during the reign of King Kalākaua.

The physical restoration of the building was begun in 1969 under the supervision of The Friends of 'Iolani Palace and the architectural guidance of the late Geoffrey W. Fairfax, F.A.I.A., and has cost more than $7 million dollars, provided by the State of Hawai'i.

At the same time, The Friends solicited money from private sources and foundations to acquire and restore the original Palace furnishings, which had by that time been scattered about the world. Meticulous curatorial sleuthing uncovered in Europe, Asia and the United States furnishings which had been in the Palace during the days of King Kalākaua and Queen Lili'uokalani.

Exhaustive scientific analyses and infinite patience were essen-

'Iolani Palace Collection

tial to enable restorers to determine the original fabrics and finishes to be duplicated on all surfaces and furnishings throughout the Palace. Carpets, draperies and fabrics of a century ago were carefully recreated, often working with minute fragments of the original material.

A total restoration of the Palace rooms with complete fidelity to the late monarchy period and adherence to the latest and highest museum interpretive standards has been achieved in cooperation with eminent conservators and craftsmen from many parts of Europe and America, coordinated by the professional staff of the Palace. As a result of this protracted and costly effort, the Palace has been returned to an extremely close approximation of its original appearance. The visitor to 'Iolani Palace may enjoy one of the most precise historic house restorations to be found in America.

Before the restoration of the Palace, in 1969, the sides of the building were covered with temporary additional offices, heavy electrical cables ran through the walls and the interior space was cut up with partitions to accommodate a functioning modern government. Fortunately, the additions were applied with care by workmen who seem to have had a special regard for the Palace, and it was possible to remove them without doing further damage to the building.

The Palace Grounds

The palace stands in tastefully laid out grounds, rainbow hued with tropical plants and flowers, and surrounded by a high stone wall. These grounds were the scene of a variety of events: torchlight processions celebrating the Coronation of King Kalākaua in 1883, an exhibition of sumo wrestling put on by newly arrived immigrants from Japan in February of 1885, numberless lū'au attended by hundreds of guests, charity garden parties such as one given to raise funds for the lepers at Kaka'ako Hospital and many other festivities.

The guests were greeted by Their Majesties, who were sometimes seated under one of the luxuriant shade trees and sometimes on the Palace veranda. They were served ice cream, cake and coffee as they strolled through the landscaped gardens and listened to music played by the Royal Hawaiian Band.

Until 1889, the Palace grounds were surrounded by eight-foot high stone walls and heavy wooden gates. In that year, the walls were lowered in the aftermath of an unsuccessful rebellion. A young part-Hawaiian, Robert W. Wilcox, led an armed party of some eighty men against the Palace, invaded the outbuildings and forced the Royal Guard to retreat to positions within 'Iolani

The Indian banyan tree on the Palace grounds began as two trees which were allegedly planted by Queen Kapi'olani around 1879. During more than a century of growth the two trees have joined together so completely that they have become one.

Photo: Hawaiian Service, Inc.

Palace itself. Wilcox's avowed aim was to restore the powers taken from King Kalākaua by the Reform Party leaders two years before. Neither the King nor the general public rose to the support of Wilcox, however, and Kalākaua allowed the volunteer militia of Honolulu to put down the Wilcox Rebellion.

Designed to protect the Palace, the high stone walls around the Palace grounds had done the opposite — had given shelter to the rebels and made it extremely difficult for the militia sharp-shooters, who had been sent to quell the rebellion, to shoot without exposing themselves. When the militia finally managed to make the open grounds untenable to the rebels and order was restored, the Palace wall was lowered to 3 feet 6 inches, topped with a decorative iron fence which is how it is seen today.

The Royal Tomb

Within the Palace grounds, a stately monkeypod tree spreads its leaves above the site of the royal tombs. In 1825 a small mausoleum was built beneath that tree to house the remains of Kamehameha II and his Queen when, after their deaths while on a visit to England, their bodies were returned to Hawai'i aboard a British warship in 1825.

During the next forty years, members of the royal family were entombed there with the bones of a number of the ancient chiefs of Hawai'i which had been brought to O'ahu from their earlier burial sites on the Island of Hawai'i.

When the Royal Mausoleum was completed in Nu'uanu Valley, above Honolulu, in 1865, the coffins were moved there from the Palace grounds, and the early tomb was demolished. A rumor persisted, however, that some remains had been left behind on the Palace grounds. To avoid any possibility of desecration of the remains of his ancestors, King Kalākaua placed a *kapu* on the site, banning anyone from entering the sacred area and had it planted with ferns and flowers. In 1930 the present fence and marker were erected.

Hawaii State Archives

The Coronation Pavilion

Although King Kalākaua came to the throne in 1874, he postponed his coronation until after the new Palace was completed. The ceremony took place on February 12, 1883, the ninth anniversary of his accession. A pavilion was built in front of 'Iolani Palace, connected to the first floor veranda by a bridge. Surrounding the pavilion on three sides was an amphitheatre which provided covered seating for thousands of spectators. The coronation ceremony was a combination of traditional Hawaiian symbolism and Christian ritual during which the King placed the jeweled crown of Hawai'i on his own head and a smaller crown on Queen Kapi'olani's. Coronation festivities lasted for the following **two weeks,** with parades, fireworks, lū'au, formal receptions and gun salutes.

After the coronation was over, the pavilion was moved to its present location and has been used since by the Royal Hawaiian Band who provided music for lū'au held on the grounds, for garden parties and for many other events. Today the Royal Hawaiian Band still performs there weekly to an appreciative luncheon crowd.

'Iolani Palace Collection

The Coronation Pavilion is octagonal in shape with eight tapered columns supporting a domed roof. Each section is decorated with a grouping of shields of Hawai'i and other countries. The copper roof, dormers and the shields have been faithfully restored. In the early part of the 20th century, the delicate woodwork of the original 1883 pavilion was replaced with a concrete basement, balustrades, and columns. These additions made the pavilion strong enough to serve as a bomb shelter during World War II and have not been altered during the recent restoration of the pavilion.

The Royal Hawaiian Band was the creation of German Bandmaster Captain Henry Berger who molded a group of Hawaiian musicians into a Teutonic military band. They paraded with the Royal Guard, played at dockside for arriving and departing vessels and enlivened royal entertainments. Berger composed the music for *Hawai'i Pono'i,* which was written by King Kalākaua and became the Hawaiian national anthem and is now the State anthem.

The Barracks

The 'Iolani Barracks was completed in 1871 to house the Royal Guard. It was designed by Theodore Christian Heuck, a German architect who also built The Queen's Hospital and the Royal Mausoleum, now known as Mauna'ala.

Originally the Barracks was located on what are now the grounds of the State Capital. In 1965 it was moved, stone by stone, to its present site in the Palace grounds.

Soon after his election in 1874, King Kalākaua reorganized the Royal Guard. He provided the men with splendid dress uniforms and equipped them with Springfield rifles.

Hawaii State Archives

The 1890 photograph above shows the Royal Guard drawn up on parade in front of 'Iolani Barracks with a battery of brass breech-loading field pieces and their mascot, at the far left of the picture.

Hawaiian Royalty Today

The destruction of the Hawaiian Monarchy in 1893 did not remove royal traditions from Island life. Birthday anniversaries of Royalty are celebrated throughout the year with band concerts and church services.

King Kamehameha I, founder of the united Hawaiian Monarchy in the late eighteenth century and Prince Jonah Kūhiō Kalanianaole, Hawai'i's delegate to Congress until 1921, are honored with State holidays. Songs extolling the virtues of royalty from the recent to distant past make up a large part of the repertory of every Hawaiian musician.

With its origins more than one thousand years in Hawai'i's past, the Royal Family has continued in leadership among the Hawaiian people and in the wider community up to the present day.

In 1966 the Royal Family returned to 'Iolani Palace as Princess Lili'uokalani Kawananakoa Morris, daughter of Prince David Kawananakoa, last heir to the Hawaiian Kingdom, became first president of the Friends of 'Iolani Palace

The Princess' daughter, Abigail Kinoiki Kawananakoa and her cousin Kapiolani Kawananakoa Marignoli (the Marchesa de Marignoli), the descendants of the late Edward Keliiahonui Kawananakoa and the descendants of the Marchesa de Marignoli comprise Hawai'i's Royal Family today.

Today 'Iolani Palace offers a glimpse into the lives of the last royal Hawaiian rulers, King Kalākaua and Queen Lili'uokalani.

The Palace is currently administered by the Friends of 'Iolani Palace under the auspices of the State of Hawai'i.

The main goal of the Friends is to operate the Palace as an educational facility, especially for the children of Hawai'i. They have endeavored to recreate the romantic period of the Hawaiian monarchy, between 1882 and 1893, and to provide every visitor, young and old, with a clear understanding of Hawai'i's royal heritage.